THE GANGES DELTA
AND ITS PEOPLE

David Cumming

Thomson Learning
New York

PEOPLE
· AND PLACES ·

The Alps and Their People

The Amazon Rain Forest and Its People

The Arctic and Its People

The Ganges Delta and Its People

Islands of the Pacific Rim and Their People

The Mediterranean and Its People

The Prairies and Their People

The Sahara and Its People

Cover: A man navigates his bicycle across the wide, green rice paddies.

Title page: Few homes in the delta have running water, so people wash their dishes in a river.

Contents page: In the delta, it is easier to get around on water than on land.

First published in the
United States in 1994 by
Thomson Learning
115 Fifth Avenue
New York, NY 10003

First published in 1994 by Wayland (Publishers) Ltd.

U.K. version copyright © 1994 Wayland (Publishers) Ltd.

U.S. version copyright © 1994 Thomson Learning

Library of Congress Cataloging-in-Publication Data
Cumming, David, 1953–
    The Ganges Delta and its people / David Cumming.
        p.   cm.—(People and places)
    Includes bibliographical references and index.
    ISBN 1-56847-168-8
    1. Ganges River Delta (India and Bangladesh)—Juvenile literature.
I. Title. II. Series.
DS485.G25C87   1994
954'.1—dc20   94-1339

Printed in Italy

Acknowledgments

The publishers would like to thank the following for allowing their photographs to be reproduced in this book: Archiv für Kunst und Geschichte, Berlin 18, 19. Mary Evans Picture Library 20, 21 both. Eye Ubiquitous: (David Cumming) *contents page*, 12, 13, 35, 40; (L. Foroyce) 29, 32; (Jim Holmes/CAFOD) *cover*, 7 top, 10-11, 11 inset, 14, 15, 16 bottom, 23, 26, 27 both, 30, 31, 39, 41, 42, 43, 44, 45 bottom left; (TRIP) 7 bottom, 9, 25, 36-7. Ann & Bury Peerless *title page*, 4, 8, 17, 37 inset. Tony Stone Worldwide (Allan Bramley) 34.
Artwork by Peter Bull (5, 16 top, 22, 24, 38, 45 top right) and Tony Smith (6, 28, 33).

CONTENTS

· T H R E E · R I V E R S , O N E · M O U T H ·

*F*rom its source high up in the Himalayan Mountains, the Ganges River travels 1,550 miles across northern India to the Bay of Bengal in the Indian Ocean. Just before reaching the bay, the Ganges meets the Brahmaputra River near the end of its own 1,800-mile journey from southern Tibet, on the other side of the Himalayas. Farther downstream they are joined by the Meghna River before their combined waters pour into the ocean through a maze of channels, both large and small. Only the Amazon River carries more water into the sea.

The Meghna is hardly noticeable by the side of the other two giants of the Indian subcontinent. The Ganges and its tributaries drain 450,000 square miles of land; the Brahmaputra, another 538,000 square miles. Together they empty an area equivalent to three-quarters of the whole of India of all its water. This water contains a lot of sediment – at least two billion tons – more than there is in any other river system in the world. It is carried down to the shallow waters of the Bay of Bengal where it is dropped, forming the largest delta in the world. The delta covers an area of 50,900 square miles (the same size as Greece). Most of it is in Bangladesh, with only a small part in neighboring West Bengal, a state in northeastern India.

Every summer, melting snow and heavy rain fill the rivers with so much water that they burst their banks, turning central Bangladesh into an inland sea. Fierce storms

These boats carry jute to factories in Dhaka, the capital of Bangladesh.

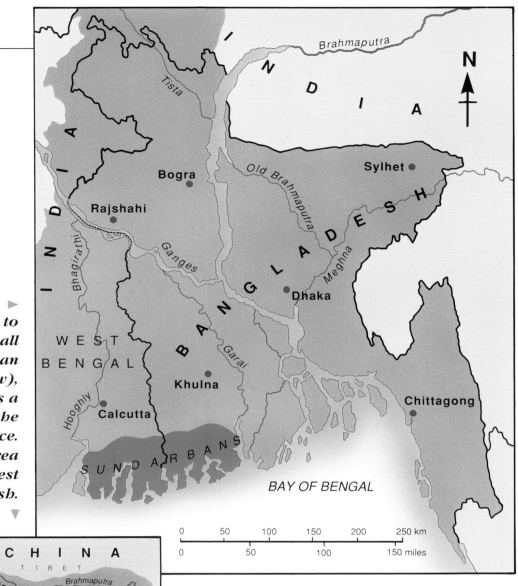

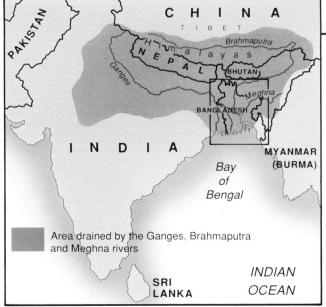

Although it seems to occupy only a small part of the Indian subcontinent (below), the Ganges delta is a huge area about the same size as Greece. The light-green area (right) shows West Bengal and Bangladesh.

Area drained by the Ganges, Brahmaputra and Meghna rivers

blow in from the Bay of Bengal, pushing huge tidal waves in front of them, which drown the coastal areas. Yet, in the winter months, there is a desperate shortage of water: the rivers shrink and the ground cracks as it dries out.

The Bangladeshis have to live with this cruel cycle of too much water followed by too little, and cope with it as best as they can. They have no option. Although they have been fighting hard for years, the battle against nature has yet to be won – if it can ever be.

5

·N A T U R A L· ·F E A T U R E S·

*T*he delta owes its existence to the rivers flowing through it, for they have brought the land on which its people live and work. Millions of years ago, there was no Bangladesh, only ocean.

Because of the way in which it has been created, the land in a delta is very flat and low; more than 75 percent of Bangladesh and neighboring West Bengal is less than 30 feet above sea level.

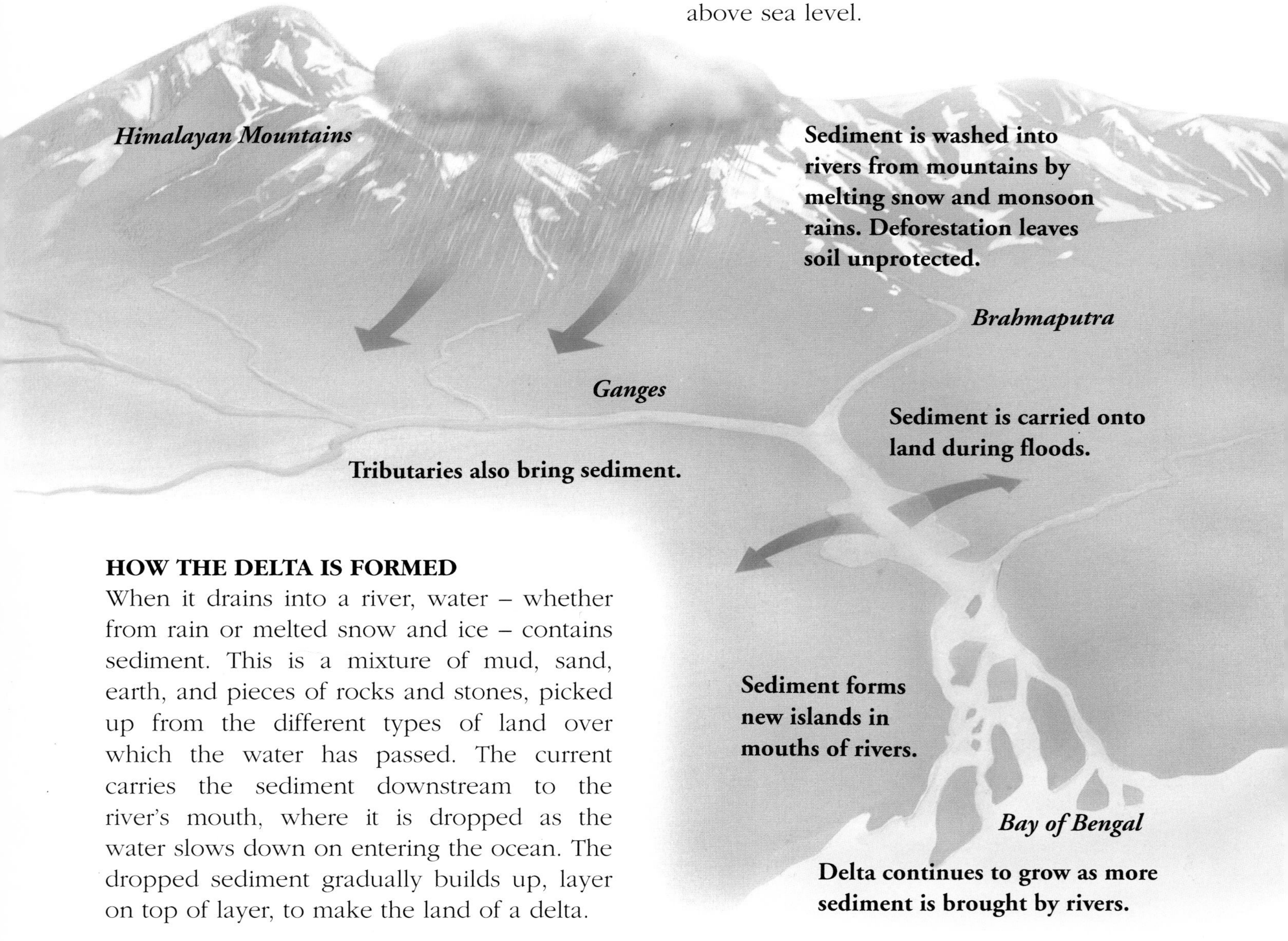

Himalayan Mountains

Sediment is washed into rivers from mountains by melting snow and monsoon rains. Deforestation leaves soil unprotected.

Brahmaputra

Ganges

Sediment is carried onto land during floods.

Tributaries also bring sediment.

HOW THE DELTA IS FORMED

When it drains into a river, water – whether from rain or melted snow and ice – contains sediment. This is a mixture of mud, sand, earth, and pieces of rocks and stones, picked up from the different types of land over which the water has passed. The current carries the sediment downstream to the river's mouth, where it is dropped as the water slows down on entering the ocean. The dropped sediment gradually builds up, layer on top of layer, to make the land of a delta.

Sediment forms new islands in mouths of rivers.

Bay of Bengal

Delta continues to grow as more sediment is brought by rivers.

The delta region is very flat and low, so villages are often flooded.

Huge banyan trees protect homes from the fierce sun and heavy rainstorms.

Not all of the sediment reaches the sea. Some is washed over the riverbanks during floods; some is deposited on the river bed, growing into islands, which clog up the mouth. But much sediment does get to the ocean, and the Ganges delta continues to fan farther out into the Bay of Bengal.

FORESTS AND WILD ANIMALS

About 10 percent of the delta is covered with forests, most of them near the coast and on the hills along its northern edge. But even the plains in between are full of trees: every house and village seems to shelter in the shade of palm, mango, or banyan trees – much needed in the summer months, when temperatures can soar above 95°F in the blazing midday heat.

In the hill forests, the leaves and branches of tall evergreen trees act like large umbrellas, shielding the soil beneath them from the heavy rain that can wash it away. This is one of the wettest parts of the world and a lot of rain can fall in a short time. In spring, the hillsides are dotted with the colorful flowers of magnolia, rhododendron, and camellia.

On the western edge of the delta and overlapping into West Bengal is the Sundarbans: an enormous soggy swamp of some 50 muddy islands covered with tropical forest and separated by hundreds of channels and creeks. Much of it is submerged by the sea at high tides, and the trees and plants have adapted to spending half their lives standing in salty water. Many have developed long, trailing roots to anchor them in the mud. Others have roots that breathe, called pneumatophores. These are spiky tubes that poke up through the mud, taking in air while the tide is out.

Many animals live in the Sundarbans, including Royal Bengal tigers, crocodiles, monkeys, deer, monitor lizards, and wild boars. Among the bird life, there are herons, cranes, storks, and snipe.

In the delta as a whole, there are some 300 species of birds. The best known are the mynah, which the local people often train to talk, the brilliant-blue kingfisher, and the fishing eagle.

Bangladesh is also home to a variety of animals, both large and small. The hills are the haunt of ponderous elephants, cheetahs, leopards, and panthers; on the plains are the gecko lizard and that fearless hunter of snakes, the mongoose. Many types of river and saltwater fish can be found in the water, along with flesh-eating turtles and crocodiles.

▲
A home in the forests of the Sundarbans in West Bengal.

An Endangered Species

▲
An increasingly rare sight today: a Royal Bengal tiger.

Hunters have nearly wiped out the Royal Bengal tiger. A national park has been set up in the Sundarbans in West Bengal to protect the remaining population, now numbering fewer than 300. Royal Bengals grow to over 9 feet long and 3 feet tall, and weigh up to 550 pounds. This is the only member of the tiger family to live in swamps, where it retreated after its natural habitat, the forests on the plains of West Bengal and Bangladesh, was destroyed. The tiger has altered its behavior accordingly, becoming equally at home in water – swimming up to 6 miles between islands – as on muddy land where it thunders along at 15 mph in pursuit of prey. It will eat fish or meat and drink fresh or salty water.

In old age, losing teeth and energy, Royal Bengals turn to easier prey: some of them turn to humans. Each year, about thirty people are the victims of these elderly man-eaters. The local people try to kill them using clay human dummies wired to batteries, which they leave in the forests. Any tiger that attacks one of these dummies is electrocuted. Since it is a protected species, the local people are allowed to trap only those Royal Bengals that are man-eaters. All others must be left alone, by law. This, however, has not kept poachers from hunting the tigers for their bones. Indian businesspeople sell the bones to China, where they are used in traditional medicines for the treatment of arthritis.

· R I C H · L A N D ·
· P O O R · P E O P L E ·

*T*he delta's land is excellent for farming. It is very flat and the soil is rich. Because of the hot, wet climate, lots of rice can be grown – so much that the Bangladeshis call their country *sonar Bangla* (golden Bengal), because of the color of the rice when it is ripening in all the fields. Today Bangladesh is the fourth largest rice producer in the world. Yet millions of Bangladeshis are poor and suffer from illnesses caused by having too little to eat.

VILLAGE PEOPLE

There are few towns and cities in the delta, but thousands of villages. In Bangladesh alone there are 70,000 villages, in which 80 percent of the population lives.

In the countryside, there are no factories providing jobs, so people can only work on the land. They grow crops for food, but also to sell for money to buy other things they need. In Bangladesh, owning a piece of land is as important as having a job is in countries that are mostly industrial.

A major problem in Bangladesh is that a small number of rich people own a lot of land, while millions of others have either very little or none at all. The landowners make up 10 percent of the population, but they own 60 percent of the land. They provide work for the people without land, either by letting them farm the land in return for a share of the harvest or by employing them for a wage when help is needed – to gather the crops, for example. Many of the landowners treat their employees badly, often paying them low wages or offering

them an unfairly small share of the harvest. While the landowners become richer, their employees usually get poorer.

Besides the large landowners, about 30 percent of the population owns land, but only a small amount of it. Religion is the main reason their farms are small. About 85 percent of Bangladeshis are Muslims, the followers of Islam. According to Islam's inheritance laws, fathers have to split their land when they die. All the children are entitled to a share of their father's land, although the daughters receive less than the sons. Farms that were once large have been broken up again and again over the

After harvesting, the ripened rice is dried in the sun, usually in the main square of the local village. Inset: Rice growing in a paddy.

generations, becoming smaller and smaller. Today, 90 percent of the farms are less than 8.5 acres. This is just enough land for a family to grow sufficient food to eat, but there is little to spare for growing crops to sell.

In a bad year, when the harvest is small, a farmer might have to buy extra food for his family. To do this, he will have to borrow money from the local moneylender. This person is usually a rich landowner who will charge the farmer a high rate of interest on the money he lends. If the farmer fails to pay back the money, the landowner can take his precious land and the farmer ends up working for him. In return, the farmer will receive some of the food he needs for his family, but he will also have to buy food in the markets. These are often controlled by the landowner who can keep food in storage so that prices rise and he earns more money. So the poor go hungry, while the landowner gets richer. For many people, life in the country becomes too much of a struggle and they leave for a city such as Calcutta or Dhaka, hoping that it will be easier there.

City Life: Better or Worse?

The biggest city in the delta is Calcutta, in West Bengal. Like many others in the developing world, it is already at bursting point, yet its population of 12 million increases daily. The new arrivals are usually young men trying to escape the tough life of a farmer. Calcutta has many factories, but they already have enough workers. Most of the men from the country end up scratching a living doing occasional odd jobs. Housing is just as scarce. If they are lucky, the new arrivals will find a home in a crowded slum. Life here is unpleasant, but it is better than joining the half a million people living on the street. Either way, whether in a slum or on the street, they may be flooded out in the monsoon and stand a good chance of catching a dangerous disease, like cholera, from the dirty water.

▶

In Calcutta, the streets are home to thousands of families. Many have come to the city from the countryside, in search of a better life.

Cholera: the World at Risk

◄ *These men do not have water in their homes in Calcutta, so they have to wash at a pump on the street instead.*

"In April 1993 we dealt with 22,000 people with cholera. We had to put them four to a bed and on the floors of the corridors. I have never seen so much suffering." This was how Dr. B.K. Das of the Infectious Diseases Hospital in Calcutta described the start of a cholera epidemic that may spread to many other countries, killing hundreds of thousands of people.

Cholera is a deadly disease of poor countries where sanitation is usually bad. It is caused by poisonous bacteria found in water containing raw sewage. Unless they are treated quickly, adults die within nine hours and children within six hours. Cholera is common in the delta – in rural areas as well as in the cities – because the waste from thousands of villages drains directly into the rivers, which millions of people use for washing and drinking every day.

Cholera has existed in the delta since the fourth century. In the present century, six epidemics have started there. The one that began in 1993 could be the worst yet. The cholera is a new type and existing vaccinations do not keep people from catching it. Thousands have already died in West Bengal and Bangladesh, and many more will die from the disease, both there and abroad. A cargo of Bangladeshi seafood that was shipped to Japan was found to contain cholera – fortunately, the discovery was made before any of the seafood was sold in stores.

TOO MANY HUNGRY MOUTHS

Bangladesh is one of the most crowded countries in the world. About the size of Illinois, it is home to about ten times as many people: 115 million in all. Roughly 3,400 people live in every square mile, sometimes even more.

Earlier this century, Bangladeshis did not expect to live long. Few reached old age, and many died young. So, even though many babies were born, the population increased slowly. Today, with better hospitals and more doctors, more people are living longer.

There is still a high number of babies being born, so the population of Bangladesh is growing every year by about 3 percent, or 3.5 million people.

Working on the land involves a lot of time and effort, and crops can be ruined by the weather. With no money for machines, Bangladeshi farmers have to rely on their families for help. The more children in a family, the more hands there are available to work the land, and the higher the chances are of there being one or two who can support the others through the bad times.

▲
Children in Batbera village. Most Bangladeshi children work instead of going to school.

This Bangladeshi mother is teaching herself to read: she was not sent to school when she was young.

Even though there are now more hospitals and doctors to treat illnesses, many Bangladeshi babies still die. One baby in ten does not reach its first birthday, and one child in four will die before it is five years old. Out of every 100 babies, 60 will be in poor health because they do not have enough to eat. When they are weak, babies cannot fight off diseases, so they die very easily. Parents have many children in the hope that several will survive childhood and live long enough to take care of them in their old age.

There is very little birth control or family planning in Bangladesh because of the pressures to have many children and because parents are unaware of the problems created by large families. Never having been to school, most of them can neither read nor write. Education is seen as a waste of time when a child can be out earning a living or helping on the farm.

Of the children who are sent to school, more are boys than girls. As a result, only 19 percent of the Bangladeshi women can read and write, compared to 30 percent of the men. This puts men in a more powerful position than women. In a Muslim country, like Bangladesh, women are meant to stay at home to take care of the family. Because they are not expected to get jobs, it is not thought necessary to send girls to school. Instead, they learn about running a home from their mothers. A daughter will copy her in the home, doing the things her mother has always done.

Boys are influenced by their fathers' behavior. In a Muslim country, men make almost all the decisions, frequently without consulting their wives. Most men want large families, in part to prove their manliness. Today 45 percent of Bangladesh's population is under 15 years old. If these children copy their parents, the population will expand faster than it is at present. Unless there are fewer babies born each year, the population of Bangladesh will double by 2023.

There are already too many people in Bangladesh. Most of them are farmers with small farms. If families remain large, the farms will become very much smaller, as they are split up when the father dies. The number of people without land will increase. People will remain poor and continue to have too little to eat.

The Farming Year

Rice needs wet soil in order to grow, so most of Bangladesh's rice is grown during the main rainy or *aman* season. The rice is sown in June or July, just before the heavy monsoon rains, and is harvested after the rains are over, in November or December. However, if the floods are very bad, much of the *aman* crop may be ruined. Many farmers also grow an *aus* crop, planted in March or April just before the "little rains" that come before the monsoon. This crop is harvested in July or August. If a farmer can irrigate his land, he is able to grow a third crop of rice, the *boro*, during the dry winter from November to April.

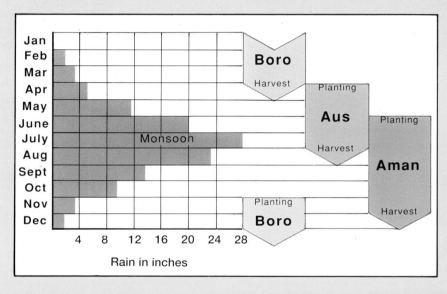

Rain in inches

▲ *Most of Bangladesh's rice is grown during the wet summer months.*

▶ *This farmer can irrigate his land, so he is planting* boro *rice in the winter.*

16

A farmer using a hollowed-out tree trunk to scoop water out of a river. He cannot afford a machine to pump it onto his rice fields.

INCREASING FOOD PRODUCTION

In a good year, there is just enough food in Bangladesh to feed everyone. But farmers are finding it difficult to grow any more than they do at the moment. Soon there will be too many mouths for them to feed.

The main food grown in Bangladesh is rice. About 60 percent of it is grown during the wet, or *aman*, season of heavy monsoon rains. Most farmers plant a second rice crop before the "little rains" that precede the monsoon. A third crop can be grown over the dry winter if a farmer can irrigate his land to make up for the lack of rain.

At present only 25 percent of the land is irrigated enough for it to be used in winter. If this area could be increased, farmers could grow more food all year round. They could grow even more food if they planted this land with modern high-yielding varieties of rice, which can produce six times the harvest of traditional types. The new varieties do not thrive in deep water, so they would be of no use in the *aman* season when floods are common. Irrigation would also help during the rare summers in which the monsoon fails and too little rain falls.

The problem with both these ways of increasing the amount of food grown is their price. Not only are high-yielding seeds more expensive to buy than traditional varieties, they also require more chemical fertilizers and pesticides while they are growing. Tube wells and diesel pumps for irrigation are even costlier. Bangladeshi farmers have hardly enough to live on, so finding money for new equipment is very difficult. Although rich landowners have the money, they are usually not interested in trying to increase the quantity of crops grown on their farms. Many of them live in towns far away from their land and spend most of their time taking care of their other businesses, which earn them more money.

·THE·DELTA· ·IN·HISTORY·

A late-sixteenth-century Indian illustration shows a new palace being built for Akbar the First. Such buildings showed the wealth of the Mogul empire.

The Dravidians were the first known inhabitants of India. Small and dark-skinned, they survived by hunting and by gathering berries and plants in the forests. Originally from the dusty, dry Deccan plateau in central India, the Dravidians moved onto the plains by the side of the Ganges River, where water was plentiful and the rich soil better for growing crops. One group, the Bangas, headed northeast, ending up in the delta. Here they established a kingdom, first called Banga and then Bangala.

In about 1500 B.C. the Aryans from Central Asia arrived in northwest India and spread across the northern plains, following the route of the Ganges. Tall and fair, they thought the Dravidians inferior and treated them cruelly. The Bangas, however, seem to have impressed the Aryans when they conquered the delta. Instead of fleeing for their lives, the Bangas adopted the Aryans' way of life and converted to one of the two Aryan religions, Hinduism and Buddhism.

The Aryans were toppled by the Moguls, another people from Central Asia, who attacked the delta in A.D. 1526. By the end of the century their greatest emperor, Akbar, ruled an empire stretching across the whole of northern India as far as Bangala. By then Bangala had become the richest Aryan king-dom, having grown wealthy through trading its rice, silk, and saltpeter. Under the Moguls, it continued to prosper: trade increased, and new cities were built with impressive forts, palaces, and mosques. Local writers, painters, and artisans were all encouraged to produce new works to demonstrate their talents and culture. Most of the population converted to Islam, the religion of their new rulers.

The East India Company had to protect itself from attacks from both land and sea.
This is the company's Fort St. George on India's southeastern coast.

EUROPEAN TRADERS ARRIVE

By the time the Moguls seized power, the sea route from Europe to India had been discovered by the Portuguese navigator, Vasco da Gama. Companies from Britain, France, and the Netherlands began competing fiercely with each other to trade with Bengal, as Bangala was renamed. Headquartered in Calcutta, the British East India Company was the most important.

As the Mogul empire broke up, the East India Company expanded into other parts of India and employed an army to protect itself from jealous rivals. After the Indian rebellions of 1857, known as the Indian Mutiny, the last Mogul emperor left India and the East India Company was left in control of most of the country. The British government immediately took over all the Company's activities and began to rule India itself.

THE DELTA IN BRITISH TIMES

The British made many changes during their rule in Bengal. One of the most important was the introduction of a tax on land. To earn money to pay their taxes, farmers were forced to grow what the British wanted to buy. What the British wanted most of all was jute, not the rice most of the farmers cultivated. So farmers began growing more jute in their fields and less rice. After harvesting, the jute was taken to factories in Dhaka and Calcutta to be turned into rope, sacks, and material for carpet backing before being sent to Britain. Under the British, farmers in the delta began using more of the land for growing crops to sell than for growing food.

Industry, too, altered under British rule. Before they arrived there were many mills in Dhaka where cotton from the hills in the north was woven into textiles for clothes. The mills were closed down by the British because they took business away from the textile factories opened in Britain during the Industrial Revolution. It was still permitted to farm cotton, but the cotton was sent directly to Britain. Some of the clothes made there were then brought back to Bengal to sell to its people.

The British were only interested in making improvements that benefited them rather than the delta's people. True, they built roads, railroads, and river steamers, but these were to make it easier to take the jute and cotton from the countryside to the factories and docks. Local people were also specially trained to work in offices and factories. Again, this was not to help them, but to make sure that everything worked smoothly for the British companies.

During British rule, Calcutta became the most important city in Bengal and, indeed, in the whole of India. India was governed from there, and it was also the main center for business and culture. The rest of Bengal developed in its shadow, including the other major city, Dhaka.

Huge sacks of raw cotton ready to be shipped back to textile factories in Britain in 1870.

INDEPENDENCE FROM BRITISH RULE

At the start of this century, many Indian politicians felt that the British were doing more harm than good to their country. They decided it was time for the British to leave so that they could look after their own affairs. The people supported the politicians and the British became so unpopular that they had no choice but to let India become independent in 1947.

At that time (as in this), the two largest religions in India were Hinduism and Islam, which had survived for many centuries. In India as a whole, most people were followers of Hinduism. However, in the northwest and northeast, there were more Muslims than Hindus. When India became independent, these areas became Pakistan, a new country split in two by 1,500 miles of northern India. In the northwest was West Pakistan. In the northeast, in what had once been eastern Bengal, there was now East Pakistan.

The struggle for independence had been a bloody one. The Indians had fought the British, as well as each other, Hindu against Muslim. Pakistan had been created to keep the two religions separate. What no one anticipated was that the people of Pakistan would start fighting one another.

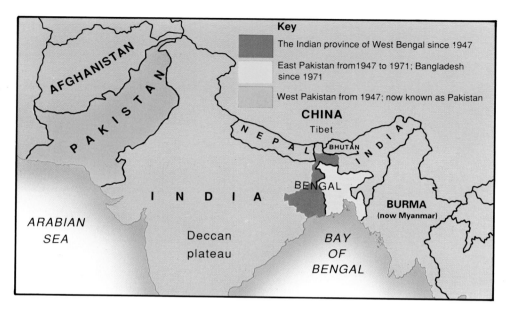

This map shows how India was split up after the British left.

BANGLADESH: LAND OF THE BANGLAS

In the same way that the Indians came to dislike the British, so the East Pakistanis soon grew angry with the way the West Pakistanis treated them. West Pakistan was richer than East Pakistan in every way. Its industries were better, as were its schools, roads and hospitals. When Bengal had been split in 1947, the richer western half remained part of India and became the Indian state of West Bengal. The poorer eastern half of Bengal became East Pakistan. West Bengal had almost all the factories but little farming land. East Pakistan was left with most of the farming land but very few factories. East Pakistan had also lost many skilled people because they were mainly Hindus who had left to live in India.

Instead of helping East Pakistan to build new factories and train people with skills, West Pakistan did everything to stop its progress. It did not share its wealth with East Pakistan and much of the money that was earned by the East was taken and used by West Pakistan.

In 1971, East Pakistan rebelled against West Pakistan and broke away to form the new state of Bangladesh (*desh* is the local word for land and the name, Bangladesh, means 'land of the Banglas'). After nearly twenty-five years of being treated badly by West Pakistan, Bangladesh was one of the poorest countries in the world. Life has changed little since then. Bangladesh has few factories. Its most important ones are connected with agriculture, processing the crops farmers grow in their fields. With few factories, the people have no choice but to work on the land, hoping that it will provide them with food and money. In Bangladesh, therefore, both the factories and the people depend on farming. All over the world, farmers are affected by the weather, but those effects are particularly dramatic in the Ganges delta where months of too much water are followed by months of too little.

· F L O O D S ·

Because the delta is very flat and low, it floods easily during the heavy monsoon rains in the summer. In a good year, only 20 percent of the land will be flooded; in a bad year as much as 80 percent. In the last century, there were 6 bad years; in this one, 14 so far. The floods in 1988 were the worst for a long time: 66,000 villages were under water, making 45 million people homeless, and at least 2,000 people drowned. The floodwater comes from three sources: the rain, the rivers, and the sea.

RAIN AND FLOODS

About 70 inches of rain falls every year on the delta. Most of it – about 80 percent – is brought by the monsoon winds that blow in from the Bay of Bengal from June right through to October. So much rain falls in these five months that all of the water cannot drain through the ground. The ground of the delta is like a giant sponge. It soaks up the rain until it can hold no more and a deepening layer of water begins to settle on top.

A school stranded by rivers flooding after the monsoon.

23

RIVERS AND FLOODS

The amount of water carried by the rivers flowing into the delta determines how deep will be the layer of floodwater during the rainy season. The rivers bring more than four times the water brought by the monsoon. The monsoon rains arrive when the Ganges and Brahmaputra are at their fullest, swollen with the melted snow and ice from the Himalayan Mountains. The rainwater raises their levels to the point where the rivers either brim over or burst through their banks, adding more water to a land already flooded by rain. The Ganges' drainage basin is south of the Himalayas, while the Brahmaputra's is to the north, so they normally reach their fullest at different times, a month or so apart. However, in some years they are full at the same time, and then the flooding in the delta is much worse.

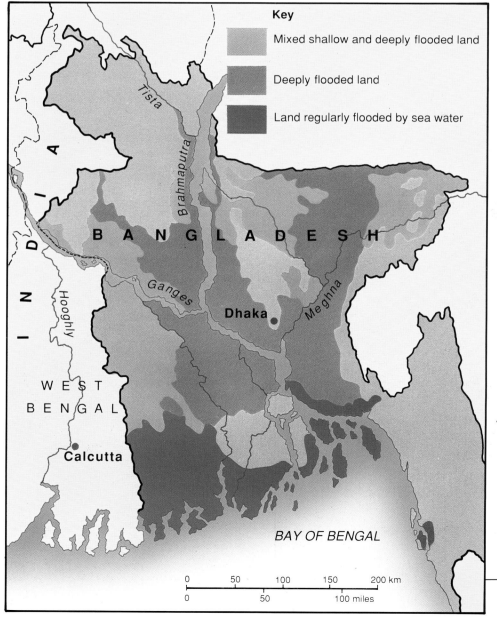

Key

Mixed shallow and deeply flooded land

Deeply flooded land

Land regularly flooded by sea water

Most of Bangladesh is flooded every summer, much of it beneath several feet of water. The areas of light green on the map show land that is least likely to flood.

Wave of Destruction

"The wind was more than 180kmh [100 mph], pushing a tidal wave over 9m [30 feet] high. It came at night, as they often do, sweeping people away while they slept. Here we must fight the sea to live," said Rafiqullah Chowdhury, a government official on Sandwip Island, recalling the tidal wave that swept across it in November 1970, killing 40,000 people. Along the rest of the delta's coast 300,000 people and 500,000 cattle died; one million were left homeless; 70 percent of Bangladesh's fishing boats were wrecked, and 80 percent of the rice crop lost.

This large ship was sunk by the super-cyclone that struck Bangladesh in 1991.

THE SEA AND FLOODS

As the inland areas begin to dry out in the autumn, it is the turn of the coast to be drowned. It is hit by cyclones. These are fierce tropical storms that form over the Bay of Bengal. In other parts of the world they are known as hurricanes (in the Caribbean Sea and Pacific Ocean) and typhoons (in the China seas). The direction in which the cyclones head is unpredictable. In some years, southern India suffers; in other years, the delta is the victim. When this happens, the hurricane-force winds of the cyclones push water up into the north of the Bay of Bengal. The narrower and shallower the bay gets, the higher the water is forced, until it builds into a wave twelve feet or more high, which is often topped by other waves just as tall. The resulting huge wave roars over the islands and lowlands at the delta's mouth, sweeping away anything in its path. Later, it retreats, dragging everything it has destroyed into the Bay of Bengal.

In the past 32 years, Bangladesh has been hit by 16 cyclones. All of them have caused enormous destruction, but the one that struck in 1991 was one of the most terrible ever. It has been described as a "super cyclone," with winds more powerful than even the biggest atomic bomb. The winds, and the huge wave they created, killed 139,000 people and made 10 million homeless.

·LIVING·WITH· FLOODS·AND· ·CYCLONES·

After terrible floods in 1988, a specialist from the United Nations Development Agency visited Bangladesh to see how floods might be prevented. He decided that floods brought more benefits than harm, and that it would be wrong to try to stop them altogether.

NO FLOODS, NO FARMING

Without floods, farming in the delta would be more difficult. As plants grow, they remove all the soil's beneficial nutrients. In most countries these are artificially replaced with fertilizers. However, in Bangladesh, fertilizers are not necessary. On their journey downstream, the smaller particles of sediment in a river are ground down, forming a fine soil called alluvium. This is full of all the nutrients plants thrive on. When a river floods, the alluvium is spread over the surrounding land, leaving a layer of rich soil after the floodwaters drop. Every year, the rivers fertilize the delta's soil – for free.

If the flooding were halted, the delta's farmers would have to buy chemical fertilizers, or their fields would soon lack the nutrients plants need. Not only are fertilizers very costly for people with little money but, when the rain washes them off the land, they pollute the rivers. In solving one problem, fertilizers would create another.

This Bangladeshi family cannot leave home because of rising floodwaters.

If flooding is stopped, the land will need fertilizers. These will add to the chemicals already being used by farmers to control pests, diseases, and weeds in their fields. Water from the fields now pollutes the nearby lakes, ponds, and swamps from which Bangladesh gets 90 percent of its fish. More chemicals will increase the chances of harming the fish and the people who eat them. Some five million people earn a living from fishing. Already they have lost money because ponds have been drained for more fields. Chemicals may now also lose them their jobs. The population as a whole will be affected since fish provide the people with most of their protein, an essential part of any diet.

◄

Chemical pesticides are used on tea plantations in north Bangladesh. Such chemicals can harm fish in the delta.

▼

FLOODS: A PART OF LIFE

In most of the world, floods are seen as a natural hazard that people have to cope with only occasionally. In Bangladesh, floods happen every year. Floods come with the rainy season; next year will be the same, and the year after that. The only thing people cannot predict is how bad the floods will be. Everyone agrees that they are annoying and destructive, but they also realize that without floods there would be nothing to eat. For centuries, people have continued to live in the delta, aware of the danger, but willing to accept the risk.

In 1988, the delta's three main rivers, the Ganges, Brahmaputra, and Meghna, reached their fullest within a few days of each other. At the point where they all meet, there was so much fast-flowing water that sections of riverbank three hundred feet wide were eaten away. The Meghna was so powerful, it changed course, opening up a new channel 65 feet wide. Land, homes, railroads, people, and cattle disappeared in a few hours. Everyone was unprepared because they had been given no warning, and many people lost everything. Nearly 70 percent of Bangladesh

The Changing Landscape

Before the Monsoon
The land of the delta is very flat and covered with the fields of small farms where rice is the main crop (1). Villages are built on the highest ground (2) in the hope that it will protect them from the floods. They are connected by tracks raised above floodwater level on embankments (3).

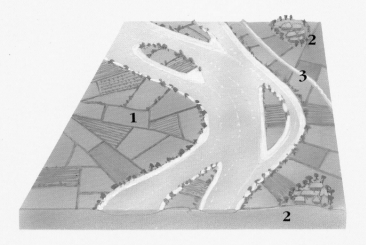

The Monsoon Season
During the heavy rains of the monsoon, the rivers swell and flood the land (4). Sometimes a river will form a new channel (5) and create further islands (6). If they are built on land that is high enough, the villages remain above the level of the floodwater, but the floods can wash away parts of embankments (7).

After the Monsoon
As the land dries out, the changes to the land brought by the monsoon are seen. Sediment left by the floodwaters may extend islands (8) and cut off sections of river, leaving lakes filled with fish (9). Although crops may have been ruined, the alluvium spread over the land during the flooding will act as a rich fertilizer. Damaged embankments must now be repaired (10).

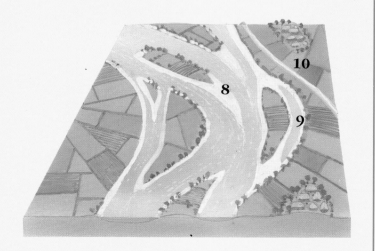

A village of bamboo houses is built on stilts to keep it above the floodwaters.

was flooded, much of it beneath several feet of water. The capital city, Dhaka, did not escape. Its streets were awash and people had to walk to work through knee-deep water. The sewers overflowed, sending dirty water and sewage onto the streets and into houses. In the countryside, farmers watched helplessly as their crops were washed away.

When the water subsided, people returned to daily life. The next harvest was one of the best for a long time.

Floods are part of life in the delta, so the people have developed ways of living with them. In areas where flooding is particularly bad, farmers grow a special type of rice with a very long stem. The grains at the top of the stem are held above the floodwater to be ripened by the sun.

Riverside houses are often built on stilts to keep them clear of danger in the monsoon. In the countryside, villages and homes are on the highest ground, connected by tracks along embankments above floodwater level. For most farmers a small boat is more useful than a cart. In the summer they can take shortcuts across drowned land; in the winter there is enough water in the maze of narrow channels for them to paddle to market. People are more accustomed to traveling on water than on land, and there are no bridges and few roads and railroads in a region where there is almost as much water as land. The rivers and their tributaries are the delta's highways, bustling with boats laden with farm produce being rowed or hauled; crowded, lopsided ferries; battered, elderly paddle-steamers; and rusty coasters.

LIVING WITH CYCLONES

The islands on the delta's coast are affected the most by cyclones. Many people live there because the soil is good for farming rice and growing coconuts, tomatoes, peppers, and vegetables such as radishes and cauliflower. There are also many fishermen, who catch the shrimp living in the Bay of Bengal's shallow waters. The fishermen's homes are simple huts made of mud or coconut matting with straw or coconut leaves on the roofs. They are easily blown away by a cyclone's winds, and easily rebuilt. The islands are low so, when the tidal waves come, there is no high ground for people to escape to. To avoid being washed away, many climb to the tops of the coconut trees and tie themselves to the trunks. The cyclones bend the trees, but they rarely break. The tidal waves flood the land with salt water, which makes it impossible to farm until the water has drained away. For many months the people have little to eat.

Many islands now have buildings made of concrete, which are strong enough to withstand high winds and tall tidal waves. The buildings are large enough to hold 3,000 people each, and they are often equipped with medicines and food. On one island, everyone was killed by a cyclone in 1970. Afterward, the government constructed a concrete building in which people sheltered during a cyclone in 1991. Everyone survived.

There are 300 concrete buildings on the delta's islands, but 3,000 more are needed. The government of Bangladesh cannot afford more. Each one costs about $120,000. Until these extra shelters are made, thousands more people will lose their lives in the cyclone season.

Floods cause Famine too

Most of us associate famine with a lack of rain, but this is not always the cause. After the floods of 1974, 300,000 Bangladeshis died of starvation. A shortage of money rather than food led to their deaths. Most were landless laborers who had lost their jobs because the land was under water. They could no longer afford to eat. Their plight was made worse when the government cut back low-priced food for the poor by 70 percent. Its stocks were low since the United States had stopped sending food aid because Bangladesh was trading with Cuba against its wishes.

▲ *Farmers cannot work the land when it is flooded, and many lose their jobs. Building mud embankments around rice fields can protect the land and crops from floods.*

· P R E V E N T I N G · F L O O D S ·

*E*veryone understands that it is difficult to control two huge rivers like the Ganges and Brahmaputra. Many people wonder if it is worth trying: with over two million cubic feet of water rushing past every second in the monsoon, they consider the rivers too powerful to tame. Nevertheless, the government of Bangladesh, helped by other countries, is trying to reduce the damage done by floods.

Since the 1960s, river banks have been raised and strengthened with concrete. However, large parts of central Bangladesh remain at risk from deep floods. In 1991 work began on the Flood Action Plan. When it is completed, thousands of miles of land alongside the Ganges and the Brahmaputra will be much safer because strong, high banks will have been built.

▶
These people are strengthening river embankments in Bangladesh to prevent their being washed away by floods.

Planting more trees on hillsides helps to keep soil from being washed away by rain.

Himalayan Mountains

Water behind dam across Brahmaputra can be released into delta in dry season.

Brahmaputra

Canal linking Ganges and Brahmaputra diverts water away from delta.

Dam across Ganges controls flow of water to delta and generates hydroelectric power.

Ganges

Canal takes water from Ganges to irrigate southern India.

Less water reaches delta in summer, preventing floods. Less sediment is brought to block rivers and mouth of delta.

Help from Bangladesh's neighbors could lessen flood damage in the delta.

Some people criticize the Flood Action Plan. They think that it will create bigger problems nearer the coast. All the water that once flooded central Bangladesh will now flood the coast, they say. So while one area has fewer floods, another will have worse ones. The critics also point out that more water going down to the delta's mouth will increase the chances of a catastrophe similar to one that happened in the 1970 monsoon. Then, the water rushing down the rivers reached the mouth at the same time that a huge tidal wave came in from the Bay of Bengal and 500,000 people drowned.

NEIGHBORLY HELP

The countries drained by the Ganges and Brahmaputra can help prevent Bangladesh's floods. If these countries built dams and canals, the amount of water reaching Bangladesh could be controlled. Less river water arriving in the monsoon season would make the flooding less serious.

The Brahmaputra comes from southern Tibet. Tibet is governed by China and, at the moment, China does not want to help. The Ganges River starts in India, and India is willing to assist Bangladesh with its flood problems. India is investigating the possibility of linking the Brahmaputra and Ganges by a canal. The Ganges would also be connected to an 18,000-mile canal network to irrigate the dry lands of central and southern India. The combined projects would divert water away from the delta in the monsoon. It is a very ambitious idea, and would take at least thirty years to complete if the money could be found for it.

Deforestation in Nepal

Deforestation of the Himalayas in places like Tibet (pictured) and Nepal allows rain to wash soil into the rivers.

In the last fifty years, 30 percent of Nepal's hillside forests have been cut down. Today 200 square miles are lost each year, while only 30 square miles are replanted. Without trees to shield the ground from the heavy monsoon rain, huge quantities of soil are being swept into the rivers and down to the delta, making floods even worse. India, too, must accept some of the responsibility, for it has been destroying as much of its own forests. The situation is made worse by the nature of the Himalayas. They are very young mountains, so they are still "soft" and easily worn away by the wind and the rain, adding more sediment to the rivers flowing down them.

Nepal, whose rivers drain into both the Ganges and the Brahmaputra, can also help. Another poor country like Bangladesh, Nepal's population has been growing so quickly that forests are being cut down at an alarming rate to obtain fuel, building materials, and farmland. An increasing amount of soil is now being washed from the land into the rivers. This ends up on the riverbeds in Bangladesh, making the channels shallower. They can carry less water, so they flood more easily.

COASTAL FLOODING

Protecting the coast from flooding by the sea is even more difficult than preventing rivers from flooding inland. Embankments are the only way of keeping the sea out. Not only must they be high enough to block tidal waves, but also tough enough to withstand the very strong winds caused by cyclones. Such barriers are very expensive. Many people argue that it would be better to concentrate on measures that would directly protect people rather than worrying about the destruction of land and property by salt water and wind.

One way of protecting the coastal people is to build more of the concrete shelters mentioned earlier. Communications would also have to be improved so that the people would be given sufficient warning of a cyclone to have plenty of time to reach a shelter. Weather satellites regularly fly over the Bay of Bengal and transmit reports back to Dhaka. Radar stations that can watch a cyclone's progress have also been built. The satellites and radar provide enough information for scientists to predict accurately how bad a cyclone is, where it will hit the coast, and when it will arrive. Although officials in Dhaka know what is happening, it is very difficult to pass this information on to the people in the path of the storm because they do not have radios, television, or telephones. Many meteorologists fear that cyclones will become even more destructive in years to come. If communications within Bangladesh can be improved, thousands of unnecessary deaths will be prevented.

▲
High earth embankments can stop rivers from flooding villages in the Sundarbans.

· D R O U G H T S ·

*I*n the summer, the delta people have to cope with too much water. In the winter, they have to live with too little. The situation is made worse when salt water enters many of the rivers and channels.

THE DYING WESTERN DELTA

The rivers in the delta often alter course. Normally there is only a minor shift, such as the cutting of a corner when a buildup of sediment blocks the main stream. At other times, there can be a major change in direction brought about by tremors or upheavals in the earth's crust. A severe earthquake in 1787 made the Brahmaputra turn south to join the Ganges (although a tributary still follows the old route, connecting it to the Meghna). Long before that, in the 12th century, the delta's land had tilted, forcing the Ganges to flow into the Bay of Bengal through Bangladesh. Previously it had traveled down what is now the River Hooghly in West Bengal, reaching the sea to the south of Calcutta.

The delta in West Bengal and western Bangladesh has been drying out ever since the Ganges changed course. Its tributaries there have become choked with sediment and weeds, with insufficient water in them to prevent salt water from being pushed farther and farther inland by the powerful tides. Watered only by the rain, the soil has lost its fertility, while the amount of salt in it has increased. It badly needs a river's nutrients to enable plants to grow in it again.

The Ganges–Kobadak irrigation project was designed to bring life back to the dying delta in western Bangladesh. Water pumped from the Ganges through a network of canals and channels would be used on more than

200,000 acres of dry and infertile land. The project was started in the 1950s and was nearly finished when the Indian government built the Farakka Dam to the north, robbing it of the water it needed. The western delta remains dangerously close to turning into a salty desert. In parts of it, the level of salt in the soil is as much as thirteen times greater than before the Farakka Dam was opened.

PUMPS AND TUBE WELLS

Across the delta, farmers have to sink tube wells deep into the ground or draw water up from the rivers with diesel-engine pumps. Few farmers can afford either wells or pumps. As a result, only 25 percent of the land is irrigated sufficiently to grow crops during the dry winter season – a huge waste when there are so many mouths to be fed.

In winter, when there is no rain, the ground cracks in the western delta. Inset: Sinking a tube well to an underground reservoir can provide water to keep the ground from cracking and allow crops to grow.

Farakka Dam adds to Bangladesh's Problems

"If salt levels continue to rise at present levels, then the western delta risks turning into a desert. Soon nothing will grow there," warned a Bangladeshi geographer recently, pointing an accusing finger at India's Farakka Dam. Opened in 1975, the dam was built to flush sediment out of the Hooghly River by diverting water from the Ganges. Less water now flows down the Ganges into Bangladesh, so more salt water penetrates farther into the delta. This harms crops and fisheries, as well as people's drinking water. The Indian government has promised to help by building a canal to transfer water from the Brahmaputra to the Ganges.

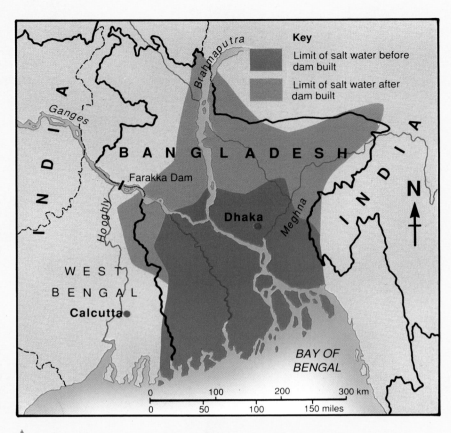

Key
Limit of salt water before dam built
Limit of salt water after dam built

▲ *India's Farakka Dam has increased the amount of salt water in the delta.*

Even when farmers have the money for wells and pumps, the water can do more harm than good because it contains a lot of salt. Though the problem is most serious in the western area, it is widespread across the delta. The reason for it is the same: during the dry season there is less water in the rivers so more salt water is able to push its way inland, some of it reaching the underground reservoirs of fresh water. By taking water from the rivers and reservoirs, farmers make the situation worse, because they are making room for yet more salt water.

There are two ways of stopping the invasion of salt water. The simplest method involves building mini-dams with sluice gates along the coast. During the heavy rains of the monsoon, the gates are left open to let the water out. In winter, they are shut, keeping the sea out of the delta and preventing fresh river water from escaping.

Alternatively, if dams were built on the Ganges and Brahmaputra, water held back in the summer to reduce flooding could be released in winter to fill the rivers and force the tides back.

· T H E · W A Y · F O R W A R D ·

*B*efore it became independent in 1971, Bangladesh was part of British India and then Pakistan. The British were interested in only what was grown in Bangladesh. They made the farmers grow a lot of jute because it was wanted by industries in Great Britain, and most of the factories they built were for preparing the jute before transporting it. The other factories built by the British were also for processing crops, such as tea and cotton, before sending them home. When Bangladesh was part of Pakistan, little changed because West Pakistan did not want East Pakistan to have industries that might rival its own.

As a result, Bangladesh has only a few small industries to make the things, such as machines, which it needs. Much has to be bought from abroad. To earn money for this, Bangladesh has to sell what it produces to other countries. Since jute has become its major crop, it is the most important thing the country can sell – in the past, nearly 60 percent of the money Bangladesh earned came from jute. Jute used to be very valuable as the only material suitable for making sacks and ropes. Now, more and more artificial materials are used, so Bangladesh cannot earn as much from jute. Cotton clothes, fish, leather, and tea are also sold abroad, but they bring the country little money because these industries are so underdeveloped in Bangladesh.

◄

After harvesting, jute is soaked in water, then taken to a factory for processing. Because of the fall in the value of jute, Bangladesh's main export crop, the country now has to find other ways to earn money.

The money Bangladesh earns from other countries is used both to supply basic needs and to build new factories. Bangladesh has to spend most of the money on basic needs, which means little is left over for factories. Because there is so little money to develop new and existing industries, the people of Bangladesh have to remain farmers. They must use the land not only to provide them with food but also as the only way they, and the country as a whole, can earn money. How much food and money they get depends on the weather. The weather can destroy all the farmers' crops, leaving them with nothing and Bangladesh with no produce to sell to other countries.

Bangladesh needs more factories. These would provide people with jobs and industries other than farming. Less would have to be bought from abroad and more things could be sold to other countries. The extra money earned could be used to build more factories, as well as new hospitals, houses, schools, roads, and railroads. With more factories, Bangladesh could become a richer country, better equipped to take care of its people. Without help from other countries, it will be very difficult for Bangladesh to prosper.

FOREIGN AID

The help given to a poor country by a richer one is referred to as aid. It can take many forms. If the help comes from only one country, it is known as bilateral aid. Help from several countries acting together is multilateral aid. Help after a disaster, such as a cyclone, is emergency aid; if only food is sent, it is called food aid. The provision of money for a particular project, such as building river embankments to reduce flooding, is project aid. If the money can be used only to buy goods and services from the helping country, it is known as tied aid.

Bangladesh receives all these types of aid every year. For example, it gets about three million tons of food aid, more if there has been heavy flooding or severe cyclones. This is in addition to the $5 billion in money, a mixture of project and tied aid, sent by governments and international organizations such as the United Nations and the World Bank.

HOW FOREIGN AID CAN HELP BANGLADESH

Richer countries can provide Bangladesh with money and machines for new factories. Businesspeople and experts can provide advice on the best way of running them.

In agriculture, foreign aid can help farmers grow more food. Increased irrigation in the winter will allow more land to be used for rice and for other food crops like wheat. The channels dug to bring the water to the fields will also act as drains in the summer monsoon, controlling where the water flows to prevent floods from ruining the harvest. Motor-powered pumps and tube wells are also needed, but few farmers can afford them. High-yielding varieties of rice are costly too, both to buy and to grow, since they require more chemicals than traditional types. If they were used, farmers could produce bigger harvests without increasing the size of their farms. The chemicals used to grow these varieties, however, can cause pollution problems, especially for the local fishermen.

More factories like this steelworks in Calcutta are needed to give people jobs away from the land.

These Bangladeshi women have been trained to take care of tube wells in their village.

Other countries can assist the Bangladeshi government in expanding the banking system so that more branches are opened in the countryside to help farmers and villagers. People can be given loans at low interest, either to buy equipment for their farms or to open small businesses such as workshops to make and repair farm equipment. The high interest rates charged by local moneylenders make this difficult at the moment.

The government can also be helped to train health and social workers who can be sent out to villages to give advice on family planning, diet, and hygiene. Given the opportunity, women can do a lot to change Bangladesh. At the moment men make almost all the decisions in towns and villages and within families. Social workers can set up women's groups where women can discuss things and be encouraged to give their opinions more openly. The groups can run reading and writing courses, as well as passing on skills that will enable women to practice a craft to earn money.

Communications throughout Bangladesh need to be improved so that goods and people can travel around more easily and warnings of cyclones can be given more effectively. More roads need to be built and the railroad system needs to be modernized.

▲
Bangladeshi mothers learn about water-borne diseases.

Does the West always know best?

▲
Two buildings in one: this cyclone shelter is also a school.

Critics of foreign aid often attack Western governments and institutions for wasting money on huge construction projects when it could have been better spent on simpler and more effective solutions. They point to the World Bank's Flood Action Plan in the delta as an example of wasted money. The World Bank is spending $5 billion to improve embankments along the Ganges and Brahmaputra rivers to reduce flooding – a massive undertaking. Many people think that it would have been better to build well-equipped community shelters on high ground and to improve communications to give earlier flood warnings. This would have been cheaper and would have saved as many lives.

Bangladeshi villagers learn about government savings plans that will help them buy farming equipment.

IS FOREIGN AID THE BEST WAY?

Many people say that foreign aid does not help a poor country like Bangladesh. They say that the richer countries often do not ask the poorer countries what they most need. As a result, money is often wasted building something that is of little use.

Any loans of money have to be paid back. If a poor country cannot repay its loans, it builds up debts, which get bigger and bigger each year. Soon it is borrowing money just to pay off the interest on the debts. Instead of becoming richer, the poor country becomes even poorer.

Tied aid, too, can harm poor countries because they are forced to buy things such as machinery from the country from which the aid comes. This machinery may not be of the type needed. It may also break down a lot and require expensive spare parts. While these may be cheaper elsewhere, a poor country is forced to buy them from the supplier of the aid.

Some of the money loaned to Bangladesh is also "tied" to the wishes of the governments or organizations providing it. If they disapprove of the Bangladeshi government's policies or plans, they will often stop the aid or reduce it in the following year. The U.S. government, for example, assists Bangladesh on condition that it does not trade with certain countries. When Bangladesh sold things to the Communist state of Cuba, the United States sent less food aid.

Much of the aid given to Bangladesh never reaches the people and places for which it is intended. Corrupt government officials spend the money on themselves and the people who vote for them. Many dishonest businesspeople steal machinery for their own factories. Others take food aid to sell in markets.

Despite all the problems connected with foreign aid, without help from abroad Bangladesh will be unable to break free from the circle of poverty in which it is trapped. It has many problems because it is a poor country, and because it is poor it can do nothing about them. Without aid, it will always remain poor and the problems will continue. Foreign aid is helping Bangladesh to help itself. Eventually, Bangladesh will be rich enough to get along without outside help.

Fish Island benefits from Foreign Aid

Although frequently criticized, foreign aid can be useful. One example is Meendwip (Fish Island), 60 miles south of Calcutta, in the Hooghly estuary on the Indian side of the delta. The World Bank is making a loan of $50 million to the government of West Bengal to turn it into the biggest prawn farm in India, providing jobs for 12,000 people. Some 2,500 fishermen's cooperatives will be based there. Cold-storage and processing plants will be built to prepare the prawns for export, which will earn India millions of dollars of much-needed foreign currency. Some of this will be used to develop parts of the island for tourism, bringing even more jobs to an area currently with none. Without aid, Fish Island would remain in its present deserted state.

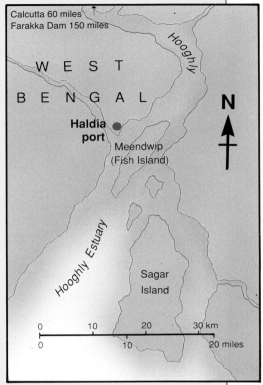

▲ *Meendwip (Fish Island) was formed from the sediment brought by the Ganges when, centuries ago, it flowed down what is now the Hooghly River. The area is rich in seafood.*

◄ *This prawn fisherman belongs to one of the cooperatives on Meendwip that will benefit from the island's development.*

G L O S S A R Y

Alluvium The fine, fertile soil that is left on the land after flooding.

Banyan tree An Indian fig tree with branches that hang down and root themselves in the ground.

Communist state A country in which the industry and agriculture are owned and run by the state. The system is meant to benefit everybody in the country.

Deforestation The removal of trees over a large area, usually to provide land, fuel, or building materials.

Delta An area of land, usually fan-shaped, formed by the buildup of sediment at the mouth of a river.

Drainage basin The area of land from which a river and its tributaries receive all their water.

Drought A long period without rain or with only a very small rainfall.

Endangered species A particular type of animal that is at risk of dying out.

Fertile When describing soil, fertile means good for farming; crops grow well in fertile soil.

Fertilizer Nutrients added to the soil to keep or make it fertile. Fertilizers are often chemicals, although there are also natural fertilizers, like animal dung.

Independence A country gains independence when it breaks away from rule by another country.

Interest Money that is paid for the use of a loan.

Irrigation The supplying of water to farmland, often by canals and ditches.

Jute A plant of East India. Its golden fibers are used to make sacks, rope, and carpet backing.

Meteorologist A person who studies the weather.

Mogul The Arabic and Persian word for Mongol, which was used to describe the family of Indian emperors started by Babur (1483–1530). He claimed to be the grandson of Genghis Khan (1162–1227).

Monsoon Summer winds from the Indian Ocean that bring rain to much of India and Bangladesh. The word is also used to describe the main rainy season.

Nutrients Minerals needed by plants to grow.

Pesticides Chemicals used to kill insects harmful to plants.

Reservoir A large lake where water is stored; underground reservoirs occur naturally beneath the earth's surface.

River system A large river and all the tributaries flowing into it. When two or more large rivers combine, as in the Ganges delta, the term describes all the rivers involved.

Saltpeter A salty substance used in gunpowder.

Sediment Small particles of earth and rock picked up from the land and carried by rivers until they are dropped when the flow of water slows down.

Sluice gate A sliding gate that controls the amount of water flowing through it.

Subcontinent A large area of land smaller than a continent.

Tremors (or earth tremors) Very small earthquakes.

Tributaries Rivers or streams that flow into larger rivers.

Tube well A pipe driven into an underground water reservoir, with a pump at the top to draw up water.

World Bank The International Bank for Reconstruction and Development, set up to lend money to countries to encourage development.

BOOKS·TO·READ

Flint, David. *The World's Weather.* Young Geographer. New York: Thomson Learning, 1993.

Harris, Colin. *Protecting the Planet.* Young Geographer. New York: Thomson Learning, 1993.

India in Pictures. Minneapolis: Lerner Publications, 1989.

Knapp, Brian. *Drought.* World Disasters. Milwaukee: Raintree Steck-Vaughn, 1990.

Knapp, Brian. *Storm.* World Disasters. Milwaukee: Raintree Steck-Vaughn, 1990.

Laure, Jason. *Bangladesh.* Chicago: Childrens Press, 1992.

Lee, Sally. *Predicting Violent Storms.* Predicting. New York: Franklin Watts, 1989.

McClure, Vimala. *Bangladesh: Rivers in a Crowded Land.* New York: Macmillan Children's Book Group, 1989.

Stefoff, Rebecca. *Overpopulation.* New York: Chelsea House, 1992.

Waterlow, Julia. *Flood.* The Violent Earth. New York: Thomson Learning, 1993.

·USEFUL·ADDRESSES·

Office of the Prime Minister of Bangladesh
Dhaka
Bangladesh

CARE
660 First Avenue
New York, NY 10016

Office of the Prime Minister of India
Lok Sabha
New Dehli
India

UNICEF
3 United Nations Plaza
New York, NY 10017

United States Committee for the United Nations Environment Program
2013 Q Street NW
Washington DC 20009

United States Department of State
2201 C Street NW
Washington, DC 20520

World Bank
1818 H Street NW
Washington, DC 20433

World Wildlife Fund
1250 24th Street NW
Washington DC 20037

INDEX

Numbers in **bold** refer to pictures as well as text.

aid 40–5
   food aid 31, 40, 44
   tied aid 40, 44
alluvium 26, **28**
Amazon River 4
animal life 8–**9**
Aryans 18, 21

banyan tree **7**
Bay of Bengal 4, **5**, **22**, **24**, 25, 33, 35
Bengal 19, 20, 21, **22**
bird life 8
Brahmaputra River 4, **5**, **24**, 27, 32–33, 38, 43
   change of route 36
Britain 19
   life under the British 19–21, 39
Buddhism 18

Calcutta **5**, 11, **12–13**, 19, 20–**21**
China **5**, 9, **22**, 33
communications 35, 42, 43
cotton **20**, 39
cyclone shelters **30**, 35, **43**
cyclones **25**, 30, 35
   and aid 40

Deccan plateau 18, **22**
deforestation **6**, **34**
delta, Ganges
   formation of 4, **6**–7
   size 4
Dhaka **5**, 11, 20, 29, 35
drainage basin **5**, 24
Dravidians 18

East India Company, British **19**
education 15
erosion of soil **6**–7, **34**

family life 14–15, 42
   and farming 11, 14
family planning 15, 42
famine 31
farming (*see also* jute, rice, *and* tea) 10, 14, 22, 30, 37, 40, 41
   and flooding 26, 30–**31**
   farmers as employees 10–11, 31
   size of farms 10–11, 15
   under the British 20

fertilizers 17, 26, 27, 28
fish 27, 39
fishing **27**, 30, **45**
   prawns **45**
Flood Action Plan 32–33, 43
flooding **7**, **23–35**
   and aid 40
   caused by rain 23
   caused by rivers 24, 26, 27, 28, 33, 34
   caused by sea 25, 30
   cities 12, 28
   coastal 4–5, **24–25**, 30, 32–33, 35
   effects on the land 27, **28**, 29, 31
   inland 4, **24**, 29, 32–33
forests 7, 9
France 19

Ganges River 4, **5**, 18, **24**, 27, 32–33, **38**, 43
   change of route 36
da Gama, Vasco 19

Himalayan Mountains 4, **5**, 24, 34
Hinduism 18, 21, 22
Hooghly River **5**, 36, 38, **45**
housing
   in Calcutta 12
   of island fishermen 30
   on stilts **29**

illness
   from lack of food 10, 15
   cholera 12–13
India 4, **5**, 12, 18–19, 20–**22**, 25, 33, 34, 38, 39, 45
   independence **21**
Indian Mutiny 19
Indian Ocean 4, **5**
industry 20, 22, 39–40
irrigation 16–**17**, 33, 36–37, 41
   Farakka Dam 36, **38**
   Ganges–Kobadak project 36
   tube wells 17, **37**, **41**
   water scoop 17
islands in the delta **6**–7, 25, 30
   formation of **6**–7, **28**
Islam 10, 15, 18, 21

jute **4**, 20, **39**

landownership 10–11, 15, 17

markets 11, 44
Meghna River 4, **5**, 27
Moguls **18**–19, 21
moneylenders 11, 42
monsoon 12, **16**, 17, 23–24, **28**, 33, 41

Nepal **5**, **22**, 34
Netherlands, the 19

Pakistan (also East and West Pakistan) 21–**22**, 39
pesticides 17, **27**
plant life 7
pollution 26–27, 41
population
   Bangladesh 14, 15
   Calcutta 12

rice **10–11**, **16–17**, 18, 20, 28
   high-yield varieties 17, 41
   long-stemmed varieties 29
   protection against floods **31**
Royal Bengal tiger 8, **9**

saltpeter 18
salt water 30, 36–**38**
sediment 4, **6**–7, 26, **28**, **33**, 34, 36
silk 18
Sundarbans **5**, **8**, 9

tea 39
Tibet 4, **5**, **22**, 33, 34
tidal waves 5, 25, 30, 33, 35
transportation 29
   boats **4**, 20, 29
   railroads 20, 29, 40, 42
   roads 20, 29, 40, 42

United States 31, 44

water shortage 5, **36–37**
West Bengal 4, **5**, 6, 8, 13, **22**, 36, 45
World Bank 40, 43, 45